The humpback whale is a giant sea creature that lives in oceans all around the world. It's a type of baleen whale and can grow as long as a school bus —about 46 to 56 feet! They weigh as much as 10 elephants put together!

Every year, humpback whales travel thousands of miles, from icy cold waters to warm tropical waters. They have some of the longest migrations of any mammal, swimming up to 5,000 miles (8,047 km) between places where they breed and where they find food.

Adult humpback whales are huge, usually about 46 to 49 feet long, but some can grow up to 56 feet! Females are usually a bit longer than males. When they're born, baby whales are already around 14 feet long and weigh as much as a small car. Humpbacks have a big, chunky body with long fins that are about one-third of their length. They have a small dorsal fin on their back, which can be tiny or a bit curved. Their mouths have special plates called baleen that help them catch food.

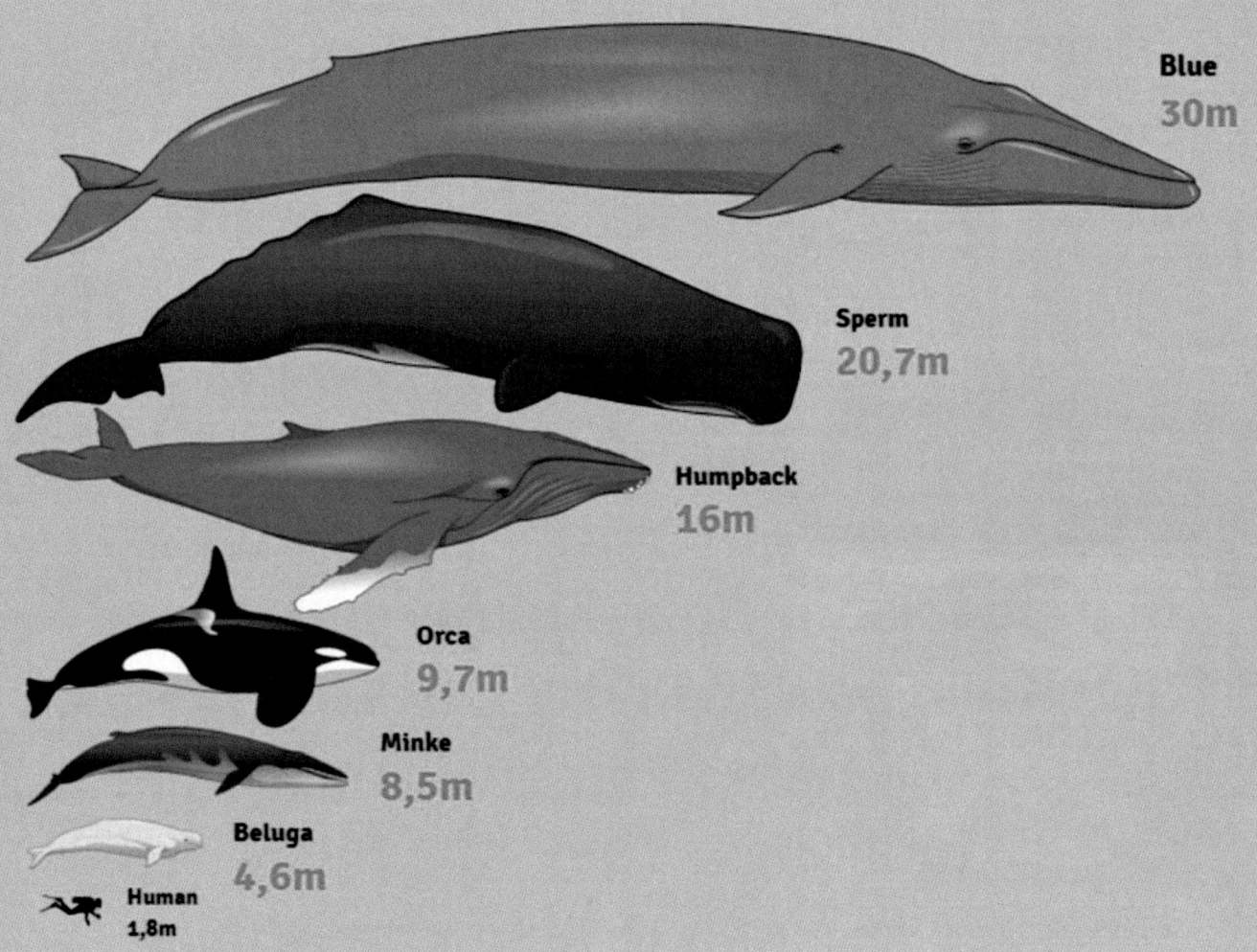

On the outside, humpback whales are mostly black on top and have white patterns underneath. Whales in the southern oceans often have more white on them. Their fins can be all white or just white underneath. Each whale has its own unique pattern of colours and scars on its tail, which helps to tell them apart. One cool thing about humpbacks is their bumpy heads and front fins, and their tails have a jagged edge. The bumps on their heads are called tubercles. They are filled with nerves and might help the whale sense things around them.

Humpback whales usually hang out in groups. These whales are very active and they might even play with other sea animals like dolphins
and big whales.

Humpback whales are strong swimmers, and they use their big tail fin, called a fluke, to push themselves through the water. Sometimes, they even jump all the way out! This is called "breaching," and when they land, it makes a huge splash. Scientists aren't sure why they do it—maybe it helps clean their skin, or maybe they just do it for fun!

They like to explore both shallow and deep waters. Sometimes they dive as deep as 2,000 feet! These dives help them find food, talk to other whales, or navigate the ocean. When they dive, they often lift their tails up high so you can see the underside.

Humpback whales eat a lot from spring to fall. Even though humpback whales are huge, they aren't predators. They don't hunt big animals. They like to munch on tiny shrimp called krill, small fish, and other tiny sea creatures. In the southern oceans, they mostly eat Antarctic krill, while in the northern oceans, they go for different kinds of krill and small fish like herring and mackerel. Humpbacks are big gulp feeders. They open their mouths wide to scoop up a bunch of food at once, then push the water out through special plates in their mouth called baleen.

One cool way they catch food is by using bubble-nets. They swim in a circle, blowing bubbles from their blowholes to trap fish in a bubble cylinder. They do this in two main ways: spiraling up or making double loops. After making the bubble-net, they swim through it with their mouths open to gobble up the trapped fish.

Scientists found out that humpback whales might learn how to do bubble-net feeding from each other, kind of like passing down a cool trick. Their flippers have special bumps that help them make sharp turns when they're catching food.

Male humpback whales sing special songs during the winter to attract mates. These songs can last anywhere from 4 to 33 minutes, and in Hawaii, they've been heard for up to 7 hours! The songs have different parts, like a musical piece with notes and phrases. Whales who hear the songs might come from far away to join the fun.

Humpback whales also make other sounds. They might "snort" to talk to their friends, "grumble" to show they're big and important, or "thwop" and "wop" to keep in touch with each other. When they're competing, they might make high-pitched "cries" or "shriek" sounds.

Orcas, also known as killer whales, sometimes hunt young humpback whales. These orcas might attack and even kill the baby humpbacks. To protect their young ones, mother humpbacks and other adult whales often stay close and try to keep the orcas away.

Humpback whales are a big reason why whale watching tours became so popular. They often do cool things on the surface, like jumping out of the water, and they aren't afraid of boats, which makes them easy to spot and take pictures of.

Whale-watching tours started in New England and Hawaii in 1975, and now the business makes $20 million every year for Hawaii! In places like New England and California, these tours also teach people about whales while they watch them.

Made in the USA
Las Vegas, NV
29 March 2025